Existential Bread

DRAG CITY

Drag City
dragcity.com

Illustrations by Griffin Trapp
Cover artwork by Ian Fullerton
Edited by Marcella Landri, Katie Gourley & Lily Oberman
Back cover blurb by Meg Coss
Layout & design by Jordan Rundle

First Edition 2024

Library of Congress Control Number: 2024938472
ISBN: 978-1-937112-43-1

For bread

I couldn't have done it without you buddy

A note about privilege

This book is about choices we make in food

The ability to make these decisions
and the education needed
to even know we have a choice
is a privilege
based on money
energy
and time

While I want people who have this privilege
to make better choices
I also want to acknowledge
that most people on this planet don't
have such freedom

We live in a system based on earned capital
where we produce enough
for everyone on earth to be fed
and we waste more than half of what we make
while people die from starvation
every day

It is time that we acknowledge
that earned capital
isn't working as a means of distribution

"Love is not only the most important ingredient: it is the only ingredient which really matters."

—Tassajara Bread Book

"Nobody knows anything."

—William Goldman

Sustainability is perfection

Perfection is an unreasonable standard
based on the assumption
that there are right things
and wrong things
It's unattainable
It's a point on the horizon
You don't have to be perfect
You just have to try
and try not to give up

I was very lucky
that my first teachers
were bad examples
They showed me
how we are all so stuck in our ways

I am also very lucky
that a larger community exists
who allowed me into their bakeries

I would be nothing
without this wonderful dysfunctional family
we call these United States

What the fuck are we thinking

The thing is

You can make bread
any
way
you
want

Bread is infinite
in variations
and scope
It defies definition

And bread
truly great bread
is made by truly dumb people
every day

Bread is a fermented food
that
in an insane alchemical way
is heated at the perfect moment
to change flour
that is virtually inedible
into one of the most nutrient-dense
and filling staple foods
that humans have ever stumbled onto

It's a ridiculous accident
that predates all understanding
of the scientific variables that define it
and arguably
in tandem with beer
is the cause of systematic agriculture

Bread making
is instinctual
if you can learn to listen
to that wonderful sense within us all
that tells us
how to make something else feel good

It is empathy
It is intimacy

If you wanna make bread
you have to learn to anticipate
something else's needs
and
if you want it to be consistent
you gotta love the way you do that
or it won't last

You have to compromise
to get what you want
I know
I know
Life is confusing
Nothing makes sense anymore
It's okay
It's gonna be okay

Bread is existential
It is not something you can make
You can only affect it

You can't just read a recipe and make bread
You have to learn how it ticks a little
or at least try to
You're dealing with living things
They want your attention
They want to be respected

If I give you a recipe
it is fundamentally flawed

I could teach you how I make bread
but that inherently rejects your circumstances
your wants and needs
and the wants and needs of
the culture and communities
that you wish to feed

So you must
learn to adjust

Bread is a great metaphor for life

If you try too hard to make something
the way that everyone else does
you will always
be thwarted
by the great
ephemeral spirit
of fuck you it doesn't work that way

Comparison
only serves to rob any practice of joy
Vulnerability
is the only multiplier of circumstances
Share your sorrow and it's halved
Share your joy and it doubles

Learn to do
and to keep doing
when all is lost
Learn how to pick up the pieces when everything falls apart
and you will never know failure again
Failure is an illusion
Your concept of perfection is the issue here

You can't figure this shit out

Life has great unanswerable questions
like
What is gluten
and how do I find love
Learn to let go and you will learn to love
Learn to let go and you will make a better loaf

Try to make the weirdest shit
that nobody's ever done before
and you'll probably make something pretty cool

Why you shouldn't listen to me

People
like my bread
cause it tastes good
and it tastes good
cause I like how I make it

I am not particularly gifted
Bread making did not come easy for me
But sometimes I think
I'm pretty smart
because I realised

that everybody
including me
is usually full of shit

I am not a scientist
I am not interested in sterile environments
or perfect conditions
Your variables will always be mysterious
There are no perfect conditions
Fermentation long predated any elements of control
But these elements are instinctual
Trust yourself
You shouldn't listen to anyone
No one really knows anything
Doubt everyone
Question everything

If you respect that the elements that define natural life
are infinite and ambiguous
you will understand
the pedagogy

It's a continuing practice

As soon as you think you know what's going on
you will be taught a lesson

Learn
to be humble
in the face of immense vulnerability
and you
will be truly unstoppable

Everything matters even if it doesn't

Personally
I wanna be a part
of an intentional community
that does the best for each other
when they can
despite the consequences

I wanna care
even if it hurts
even if it's hopeless

I don't wanna punish myself for caring
My intention is to do the best
not just for me
but for everyone around me
because despite
whether or not it works
that's the world I wanna live in

While sometimes
I'm trying to find that line
between community
and being left the fuck alone
I think it's important to challenge ourselves
to envision the world we want
and work towards it in everything we do

I hope you can learn
from my experiences
the way that you wanna make bread
a way that makes you happy
at least some of the time

People will taste that
Your happiness
Your practice in engagement
with joy and vulnerability

These are the most important ingredients
Once you have them
You can feed your culture

What I'm saying is
there's no mastery
of this process
any more than there's a mastery of love
You can only break down walls within yourself
Fall into it
and feel everything in time

Bread isn't like life
It is life
It's a living thing
The variables you're affecting
are the variables of the world
at large

It's not black and white
But
you need to make choices
Doing nothing is a choice
so do something

try
    try
        try
Try to make the world a better place
or at least a place with better bread

But first
try
to understand

Why I do everything so weird

I make bread with whole grain flour
I go far out of my way to ensure
that all of the grain is used

But most whole grain things
are not what you'd think

I'd think
that you'd think
that they were actually
100% whole grain
But
they're not
There's actually
very little standard to that

Also I make bread
exclusively
with a natural leaven
commonly known as sourdough
Yet most bread isn't sourdough
even if it's labeled that way

Maybe you're starting to see a pattern here

I also make single origin breads
Breads that have one variety of grain
so that you can actually taste
what is einkorn
what is rye
what is wheat

I also
go very far out of my way
to make local bread
using local ingredients
because I think
that local is ethical

The thing about the way I do things
is that it shouldn't be weird

Things should be local
they should be ethical
and there should be more
actually whole foods

All those things are more direct
minimalist practices
with less infrastructure
that create less waste

I do everything this way
because
it makes everything inconsistent

Like loving anything
it's a process of adaptation

You find yourself changing
to please something
or
trying to change something
to meet your needs
and maybe that's not healthy
or sustainable
but it seems to be inevitable

You can love something for what it is
for only so long
and then you have to find it
again and again

Cause it does matter

I think bread is important
because of its history
its possibility
and how just like anything
to succeed
you only need to figure out
how to get out of your own way

What makes me get out of my own way
is understanding
how I can instill care
and love in my community

How I can save the world
one loaf at a time

So I decided to make
whole grain sourdough
with locally sourced grains

All these things
help me think more carefully
and be intentional
about what I do

Like each word in a haiku
I want to be tender
romantic about everything

In the end
that's just the way I like it
I like making bread
and I like what it makes of me

I do it because I love bread
and I feel like bread loves me
for all the things I can and cannot be
and no matter who I am today

I can come to it
and feel it
feel pleasure
and pain

That gives me meaning
on my better days

Why cookbooks and bread don't mix

This book isn't about
how to make bread
cause there isn't
one way

The point of this book
is not to teach you how to make bread
but to connect you to bread in a deeper way
To send you down the rabbit hole
so you know what it means to make bread
So you can decide
what you wanna know
about bread

I can't teach you how to make bread
All I can teach you
is how I have seen others make bread
and how I make bread
That is all I have to give
My engagement
My practice

There are so many variables in bread
and especially with sourdough
and local flour
there's just no way
that two people can make the same loaf
in two different environments
no matter the precision
or attention to detail

Everything about you
and your intentions
affects what you make

That's what's really wonderful about making food

What makes the best bread is letting go

What makes the best food is you
loving the process

Make food the way you love
and you're nourished
as much by the process
as the food itself

I want you to understand
this isn't a recipe
it's a practice

Bread makers don't really use recipes
They use **baker's percentages**
This is a formula
where everything
is a percentage
of the total amount of flour used

like this:

100% flour	2.6% salt	20% starter
70% H_2O	30% milk	

The flour is the base of the formula
cause it's the most common variable

The sum of the ingredients
won't add up to 100%
All the other ingredients' percentages
are relative to the flour

If you used
1000g of flour
you'd need
700g H_2O
26g salt
300g milk
200g starter
according to the previous percentages

This way
the recipes can be easily scaled
to make one loaf
or one thousand

The one exception
is that I adjust the salt
as a percentage of the water in the recipe
to 3%
This is because I'm a silly hippie
and I like the idea that sea water is roughly 3% salt
To me it feels natural
and harmonic
and frankly
it works

We need to talk about expectations

If you want your bread to look like the picture
you saw of someone else's bread
you're making an art project
If you wanna feed your family
you're making food
Pick a lane
and learn to adjust your expectations

There's no such thing as a professional baker
Capitalism shouldn't define you
The customer isn't always right
The customer doesn't exist

Bakers don't have to get up early
Bake whenever the fuck you want

Gluten isn't what you think it is
and your bread is good bread
no matter what it looks like

The worst bread you ever make
will still be incredible bread
and your mom will be proud of you

You don't need your father's approval
He doesn't understand you

But why should I

Why whole grain

Whole grain bread is special
Something ineffable
misdefined
lost in semantics
and some small conspiracy

Whole grain bread is hard
It's a challenge
It goes against the norm
The techniques are unsettled
The infrastructure is against you

In the end it's actually simpler
but a lot of unlearning needs to happen
to get to that point

It's like the doing the right thing "thing"
It's always more difficult
to find the noble path
of embracing conflicts
and rejecting aggression

We are fear machines
doomed to anxiety
cause we don't get chased by bears anymore
so violence
and reductionism
are our first instincts

Whenever I hear
"that's just the way we do things"
I find myself
looking for a better way

How we process foods
makes very little sense
We discard so much
of what's actually good for us to eat

In this case information is annoying
cause it's pretty circuitous
and different people
mean different things
when they say the same words
but the important part is
what we're doing to grain
doesn't make any sense

There's very little good reason
to discard any part of the grain

Once I understood
what whole grain bread
actually could be
it seemed like the only answer

Why sourdough

First things first
bread doesn't make you fat
and there's no such thing as a carb
There's only grams of carbohydrates
and if you didn't eat any of those
you'd die

When we ferment grain
the yeast converts starches into sugars

The yeast consumes the sugars
and they produce gas as waste
The dough fills up with these yeast farts
until we bake it
resulting in bread

Sourdough is the way bread has been made
for 10,000 years
by conservative estimates

Sourdough or naturally leavened bread
is made with a sourdough culture
or starter
A sourdough starter
is made up of a diverse group
of millions of yeast and bacteria

A packet of yeast
you buy in the grocery store
is only made up of one very particular strain of yeast
Known as monoculture yeast
or commercial yeast
Monoculture yeast works faster
and more consistently
than sourdough

Using monoculture yeast
Started in the early 1900s
right about when food started to be industrialized
and bread started to be seen as unhealthy

We start to see
how bread went from being a staple food
to being considered so inflammatory
with the advent of monoculture yeast

Sourdough's longer fermentation
and its diversity of yeasts and bacteria
has some crucial effects on making bread digestible

The bacteria in a sourdough starter
breaks down phytic acid
and makes nutrients
that are otherwise unavailable
bioavailable
It makes insoluble fiber soluble
and digestible for its nutrients
and not just passable matter

In case you didn't catch that
I was talking about poop

It's currently believed that most grains
are inflammatory to the digestive and vascular system
but with the longer fermentation process of sourdough
the inflammatory elements are predigested
and seemingly harmless

Sourdough fermentation
also makes the sugars in grain
more complex
so that they give you long lasting energy
and don't cause insulin shock

The lactic acid in sourdough is a preservative
and in a vacuum
sourdough bread made of just flour and water and salt
will never mold
only go stale
and even then at a reduced rate

And producing monoculture yeast
on the scale that we do
and shipping it around the world
is another huge industrial process
that uses a lot of energy and infrastructure

You can make bread with commercial yeast
You can even spike your naturally leavened dough
with yeast
I will not be mad
I will just be disappointed in you
But I am not your father
and I never will be

Why local

Well
cause it makes sense

The goal of everything I work toward
is less
cause that's more efficient

I want less stuff
and more care
in every part of my community

I want a say in how my grain is farmed
I wanna vote
on what they do
and how they treat every being
on every level
that participates in this cycle

Grain is 75% of the world's agriculture
It is the first step to affect global politics
Most of the focus in the U.S.
in terms of ethical eating
has been on veggies
which is 3% of U.S. agriculture

Grain is the biggest part of our agricultural system
and defines everything we do

If we can change the way people think about grain
we can change the way the world works

I wanna participate in my local grain economy
to support local farms
developing accountability
and community

Making our community intentional
is one of the only ways I know
to directly shape lasting change

I want good farming practices
to go into our food
Sustainable practices
Regenerative practices
Practices that add nutrients back to our soil
that is growing more and more deficient every day
heading towards a tipping point
where we might not be able to grow enough food
to feed our population

Working with local farmers
also allows access to varietals
that would never be grown
or processed by large corporations

due to the lack of infrastructure
around their processing
and lower crop yields

This gives me access to flavors
that would otherwise not be available
in profit-driven models

Profit-driven models also fail to
support regenerative farming
where the land is not just rotated and rested
but where synergistic plants are grown
in specific patterns
so that we can replenish
the nutrients
that the previous crop
took out of the soil

It's really crucial
to try to use everything
in the rotation
of regeneration
of growing grains
in my community
because that enables the land
and the life it supports
to thrive

I like to bake with the grain I have
not the grain I want
But that ends up being the grain I want
It challenges me to use all sorts of flavors
that are unique
and beautiful
and so fucking wholesome

What are you gonna put in your bread

Grains

Water

Stuff

Well first

What the fuck are grains

Grains are seeds
typically of grasses
They are made to germinate
or sprout
into new plants

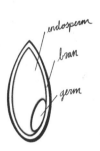

Grains are mostly cereals or legumes
but we're mostly gonna talk about cereals

They have a protective casing
called the **bran**

Bran is where a lot of the nutrients are in cereal seeds
but the bran also contains phytic acid
an antinutrient
which stops you from absorbing certain nutrients
The bran is the armor that protects the seed
from breaking down
typically from rain
but also from the saliva in your mouth

You can't inherently digest all the nutrients
in the bran
through consumption
so eating whole grain things
that aren't fermented
is just increasing fiber
and not necessarily nutritional content

Then we have the **endosperm**
just inside the bran
the white starchy part

Endosperm is the nutrient package
to feed the growing embryo inside the wheat seed
It's everything the embryo needs
for development

In wheat
this part contains two proteins
glutenin
and gliadin

Glutenin has a rubber band effect
It's tough and chewy
responsible for the pullback
or elasticity of a dough

Gliadin is the stretchy part
responsible for the extensibility
or extendibility
or the ability to stretch
without tearing

When water is mixed with these proteins
it forms **gluten**

Deep inside the endosperm
is the embryo of the seed
the **germ**
in the case of wheat being selenium
or vitamin E

This is the fat in grain

Now I don't know what you've heard about fat
but I believe that it is a very important part of a healthy diet
and also the means by which flavor travels

This is where we get into history
Why are the parts of the grain
traditionally separated
and discarded
and how do we get them back together
in their integral state

Well
I'm so glad you asked

Once upon a time
everything was stone milled

Stone milling is simply the grain passing
between two stones
one of which is moving
so the grain is crushed
and comes out the other end as flour

When the flour came out
the bran was typically sifted off
because the bran was thought to be inedible

As technology developed
we got better at sifting
and bread got whiter and lighter and fluffier
but the germ was hard to separate

But through many years of ingenious research
and corporate espionage
a type of milling called roller milling was pioneered
and this quickly became the world standard

The process of roller milling
separates the bran
germ
and endosperm
nearly perfectly
so that the fat
which is also the only element of wheat that spoils
could be discarded

But even now
that we know
that all of the grain is edible
nutritious
and delicious
we still discard most of the bran and germ

Flour
almost exclusively
is still roller milled
and even if it's labeled whole grain
has been separated and reconstituted
to approximate
apocryphally
the original content of the initial seed

In my world
whole grain flour
is only whole grain
when the grains go in the mill
and all of the flour
comes out of the mill
at virtually the same weight
without being filtered
or reconstituted in any way

But this is actually quite rare

Whole grain and stone milling
is mostly a thing sought out
by weirdos with enough time and energy
to sort these things out
and ensure the integrity of these standards

The funny thing is roller milling
and discarding so much of the grain
uses tons of energy and immense infrastructure
and is inherently wasteful

It's just that it's been done this way for so long
the infrastructure around milling
and baking is stuck in the idea
that people don't want whole grain flours

But most people have never had whole grain flour
only poor substitutes
They don't know whether or not they would like them

They're robbed of the choice due to an industry
stuck in repetition

Outside of outdated assumptions
there's no good reason
we make so much white flour
and white bread

And to me
in the face of global warming
starvation and global poverty
it's crazy that we go so far out of our way
to separate the parts of flour
and throw so much of a food away
that we spent so much energy growing

How do I know what's in my flour

Just like with whole grain
there is very little integrity
or consistency
to the definition of different types
or labeling of flour

But generally
sifted or bolted flour
is when part
or all
of the bran and germ is removed

The miller may speak about extraction rate
or ash content
which should tell you
relatively
how pure the flour is

Higher ash content
is more bran
Higher extraction rate is more of the total grain

In general
local millers will try to preserve the germ
even if they're sifting off the bran
whereas big conglomerates
always throw away the germ
even if they say they don't

Their products sit on grocery store shelves for years
and they are worried about spoilage

"Nice"

This includes "nice" flour brands
that are named after sweet old men
and chivalrous knights and kings from days of yore

A lot of commodity mills will age
or chemically affect flour
to bake more consistently
and have a more uniform color
This is called bleaching or bromating

All flour grown by farmers
taking certain subsidies from the U.S. government
is mandated to be enriched
with powdered vitamins and minerals
the idea being that it makes flour more nutritious
but actually the nutrients that are added
are the same nutrients that get taken out
when the bran and germ is removed

All flour is all-purpose
All flour is bread flour
These terms are talking about protein content
but they have very little consistency
when it comes to a baking practice

Bread flour is typically high protein
all-purpose is lower in protein
and cake flour
the lowest

There are bakers all over the world
who make great bread
out of low-protein
or even gluten-free grains

The theory of gluten
is that if these proteins are stressed
and then allowed to relax
that they will be able to stretch further
and thus the structure of the bread is defined

In North America
high-protein flour
tends to be around 13–20% protein
whereas in Europe
where Americans go
and rave about how amazing the bread is
protein contents are rarely over 13%

Something like gluten probably exists
but it's very unclear just how much stress and relaxation
these proteins need to function as elastic
So it's still not helpful to think about what gluten is
cause there's actually no consensus
except by anecdotal evidence
through generations of bakers baking

If you don't wanna be driven crazy
try to forget about protein
You'll be a lot happier

Everything that has a cell has protein in it
If you really wanna be healthier
eat a vegetable for once in your goddamn life

The thing to remember is the lower protein a flour is
the less it wants to be hydrated and mixed
The higher protein a flour is
the more hydrated it wants to be
and the more it wants to
or can be mixed

Usually the more protein a grain has
the less starch content
and vice versa
the idea being that a grain
with more protein is suited to bread
and a grain with more starch
is suited to pastry

Another flour statistic you might run into
is the falling number

Falling numbers are the result of a test
that helps identify the structural integrity of the starch chains
Falling number measures the amount of pre-harvest sprouting
that occurs in the grain
while on the stalk in the field

It helps determine whether the grain has been damaged
by rain or other factors before harvest
When wheat gets wet before being harvested
it can start to break down
and release a type of enzyme
This enzyme can affect the quality of the flour
made from that wheat

Sprouting grains is a process
where grains begin to grow into plants
after being exposed to moisture and warmth
This is also known as germination
When grains sprout
they undergo various changes
that can make them more nutritious
and easier to digest
just like with sourdough bread
Sprouting grains make the sugars less harmful
the proteins less inflammatory

and the nutrients in the bran more bioavailable
It's important to note
that sprouting requires careful handling
to prevent the growth of harmful bacteria
and it uses a lot more water and time
than making sourdough bread
which achieves the same result

But sprouted flour or grains
can be a nice way
to add flavor or texture
to your bread

How do I source local grains

Growers of local grains are a community
that at its core is at odds with the way we source our foods
For the most part you won't find local flour at your grocery store
but you could try poking around in the bulk section
especially at a co-op

I'd say the best way to find local grains
is talk to a local baker
Snoop around for a baker who uses local flour
or talk to your friends who bake

It tends to be a process of ebb and flow
There are lots of local farms
and they don't always know how to communicate
so there is a vast
disjointed network
of small mills and farms
who aren't always aware of each other
and sometimes

they will even source things from places
that you might not be comfortable with
so make sure to ask questions
about where everything actually comes from
and how it's processed

If you live in the Midwest
there is a network of local farmers
millers
bakers
and brewers
called the Artisan Grain Collaborative
and there are similar networks all over
like the Northeast Grainshed Alliance
the Common Grain Alliance for the the Mid-Atlantic
the Colorado Grain Chain
the California Wheat Commission
and numerous others

What the fuck is wheat

Wheat is a grass widely cultivated for its seed
Wheat is grown on more land area than any other food crop
World trade in wheat is greater than for all other crops combined
Globally it is the leading source of vegetable proteins
in human food
What we usually think of as wheat
is flour
ground from the seed heads
commonly called wheat berries

Wheat is also grown in different seasons
resulting in important variations
for land management
and baking qualities

There's winter wheat
sown before the winter and harvested in the spring
and spring wheat
planted in the spring and harvested in the summer
These are the two most common growing seasons
however there are such things as summer and fall wheat

What is GMO

While years of breeding on farms or even in labs
enabled genetic modification
much of what we hear about as GMO
is actually lab modification of grains at the genetic level
This is an issue in corn and many other crops
but it's not widely practiced in wheat yet
The first GMO wheat
actually entered the market two years ago
and is not very commonly used

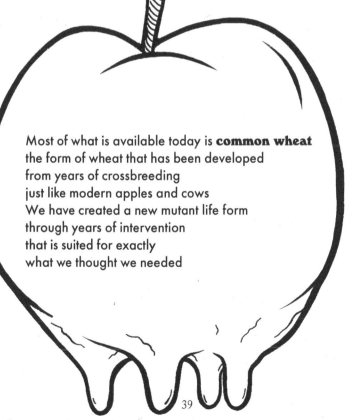

Most of what is available today is **common wheat**
the form of wheat that has been developed
from years of crossbreeding
just like modern apples and cows
We have created a new mutant life form
through years of intervention
that is suited for exactly
what we thought we needed

There are older versions of wheat
varietals with different characteristics and flavor
generally called **heritage grains**

There are hundreds of varieties of heritage grains
more than I can go through here
What's important to remember
is that heritage grains
while expensive
due to overall lower yields
are beneficial for farmers
and the environment
cause they tend to have more genetic diversity
deeper roots which capture more carbon
from our air
and are less susceptible to disease
and crop failure

Among these varietals are different color wheats
The brown flour that you most commonly see
is **red wheat**
The tannins make the flour red
But there are **white wheats**
and **yellow wheats** with no tannins
There are also **blue**
purple
and **brown wheats**
which contain different amounts of anthocyanin
a powerful antioxidant
but unfortunately
currently in the U.S.
only red and white are widely available

Some farms are now also developing
population wheats

Population wheats are various varietals
that are sown together in the same field
Over the years
what grows
becomes the next year's seed blend
and so on
so that after a few years
the seed mix is ideally suited
to that specific farming environment

And there are ancient grains

What the fuck are ancient grains

Ancient grains
are just ancient varietals
or species of grains
Grains like einkorn
emmer
and spelt
are still wheat
They are less available
and cost more
just like heritage grains
because through typical farming practices
they have lower yields
and ancient grains
typically need to be dehulled

Unlike common wheat
where the husk
that surrounds the seed
flakes off easily
ancient grains have a hard inedible husk
that needs to be removed before milling

Many of these ancient grains
are early forms of wheat
Emmer and einkorn are the earliest types of wheat
but all modern forms of wheat
are related to emmer

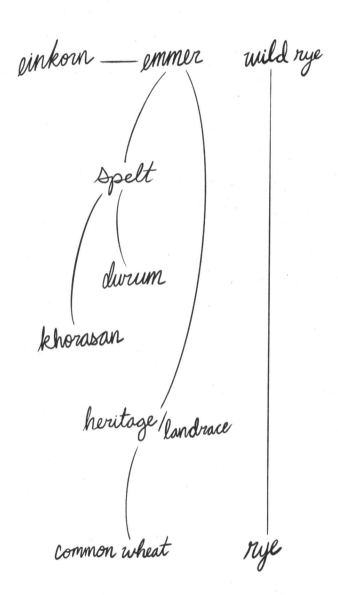

einkorn — emmer   wild rye

spelt

durum

khorasan

heritage/landrace

common wheat   rye

Einkorn

Einkorn wheat was one of the first plants
to be domesticated and cultivated

Einkorn has a knack for adapting
to challenging conditions
It grows well in hot and dry
or cold and damp environments
even tolerating soils with high salinity
and like many heritage wheats and ancient grains
has deeper root structure
which benefits soil health
and sequestration of carbon

Einkorn has a beautiful color
on a spectrum of bright yellow to beige
cause it's rich in a carotenoid called lutein
and more protein and fat
than other forms of wheat

It tastes
when cooked
like butter
It is
in short
the shit
I love einkorn so much
it hurts sometimes

Einkorn has only 14 chromosomes
compared to 42 in modern wheat

Emmer

Emmer has an earthier more tannic flavor

Emmer is very low in typical bread-making proteins
but can make wonderful bread
with a little extra care

Emmer has 28 chromosomes
compared to modern wheat
which has 42

Spelt

Spelt is the youngest ancient grain
Spelt is very extensible
and has less elasticity
due to being more rich
in gliadin than glutenin
It's also sweeter
and grassier in flavor

Durum

Durum is an older variety of wheat
but not quite ancient
Bright yellow in color
due to an immense amount of beta carotene
Durum has tons of protein
but is low in gluten-forming proteins

Durum is usually known as semolina
which is a term for coarsely ground durum flour
typically used to make pasta
or couscous
It makes a very chewy dough
Durum has tons of elasticity with less extensibility

Where durum is grown in Italy
they make a bread called Pane di Altamura
that's known for its fluffy open texture
and its incredible keeping quality
This is partly because of sourdough's preservative quality
but also because durum flour
when baked
actually seeps water as it ages
so rather than staling
the bread maintains its moisture content

It has a rich fruity taste
reminiscent of olive oil

Kamut

Kamut is copyrighted
which is ridiculous
Khorasan is the generic version
not grown on the specific farm
that owns the copyright

Essentially
these two grains
which are only different in name
are a type of ancient wheat
similar to durum in color

hardness and flavor
but the berries are slightly longer

Kamut was discovered
and redeveloped to be a staple crop in Montana
by a farmer who thought he had found the holy grail of grain

He copyrighted the seed to protect it
from large shitty farming corporations
but only succeeded
in making the grain less accessible
and confusing
to the local farming and bread movement

This grain is delicious and has wonderful qualities
although it's principally grown in Montana
on one farm
and I live in Illinois
so I stay the fuck away from it

Rye isn't really rye

There's something here
about the integrity of definitions
that I don't quite wanna get into
but the short version is I went from a world
where people said that's not punk
to a world where people said that's not pumpernickel
and no one knew what they were talking about
in either context

Things tend to lose meaning
especially when you take them seriously

Rye is different from wheat
It's not a type of wheat
It's in the same family
but it's different
like that cousin you have who never talks at Christmas

Rye relies on something different
to make fluffy bread
called pentosans

Pentosans are a type of complex carbohydrate
that can be found in the cell walls of plants
Present in grains like wheat
rye
barley
and oats

In grains
pentosans contribute to the overall strength
and flexibility of the plant's cell walls
so in baking when they absorb water
they act a lot like how we imagine gluten does

Rye likes it fast and hot
to get a fluffy crumb
and not be gooey
or collapse while baking

Typically bread
made from exclusively rye flour
wants to be baked at a very specific dough temperature
and a very specific acidity
in order to get a good rise and an open crumb

There's a great book about rye
that talks about various rye-baking techniques
called The Rye Baker

Rye bread can also be made into a very nice
albeit dense
sort of brick of a bread
if you don't wanna think about it too much
and enjoy eating bricks

Rye bread as we know it in North America
has very little to do with any actual rye flour
The flavors we know as rye are actually spices
typically caraway
coriander
onion
fennel
and anise

Rye bread in North America
is usually
mostly
if not all wheat
although
these breads are often supplemented
with cornmeal
or dried bread crumbs
to make the texture more
like European rye breads
made with larger portions of rye

Which is pretty silly
because the same effect can be achieved with
you guessed it
actual rye

Rye can be difficult to work with
It makes doughs more sticky and clay-like
even in small percentages

Rye also increases caramelization
due to its abundance of available sugars

Rye also has more mineral content which
speeds up fermentation
and drinks up water like nothing else

Triticale

Triticale is a hybrid of wheat and rye
50/50
first bred in laboratories during the late 19th century
in Scotland and Germany
It is more commonly available in Europe and the UK
but has a lot of great applications in baking
It is also a beneficial crop for land management

Corn isn't really corn

Maize used to be a wild grass called teosinte
and was bred into what we know it as today
much how common wheat used to be einkorn

Corn is actually an old term
for small particle
or almost any grain
This makes studying grain history endlessly confusing

Let's get this straight
Maize is maize
not corn
and maize is a grain
The "sweet corn" we're used to
is a modern mutant
but there is incredible variety within maize
The larger part of the family is a drier kernel
that needs to be milled
and hydrated
and cooked to be edible
and maize has its own unique process
much like sourdough
to make it more digestible
called **nixtamalization**
In nixtamalization the maize is treated with an alkali solution
to break down its anti-nutrients and increase its niacin content
This also makes the dough taste smoky
Most maize made into tortillas or tamales
is processed this way
and the dough is called masa
or nixtamal
or dried as masa harina

This process
was already being practiced
from the tip of South America
well into Canada
when early colonists arrived to the Americas

Grits are typically a type of maize called dent corn
because of the dents on each kernel
Dent corn is treated with lye
and it swells up
into what we know as hominy

The large kernels are then dried and ground roughly to make grits
but often in the northern U.S. coarsely ground untreated maize
is also sold as grits

Cornstarch is simply the endosperm of maize
much like what sifted or white flour is to wheat

Buckwheat

Buckwheat isn't a cereal
but a pseudocereal
actually the seed of a flower
in the same plant family as beets
But buckwheat has a cereal-like structure
and an intense
almost chocolatey flavor and bitterness
In Asia and the northeastern part of North America
tartary buckwheat is more common
Tartary buckwheat looks different
more like wheat berries
and has a milder flavor

It is often toasted and cooked whole
and called kasha

Because buckwheat is a legume
it's also a nitrogen fixer
meaning it grabs nitrogen from the air
and puts it back in the soil
So it's very valuable
in regenerative crop rotations

Millet and sorghum

Millet and **sorghum** are grains
commonly called finger grains
because of the way they grow off the stalk in clusters
that look like fingers
The seeds are little spheres

Millet has a warm mineral-rich flavor
reminiscent of sweet cream butter
and salt

The stalk of sorghum is made into a syrup
that is nearly identical to molasses

While millet and sorghum are a very delicious
and less impactful to soil quality alternative to wheat
they are quite high in the anti-nutrient
known as goitrogens
which interferes with the normal function
of the thyroid gland and effects metabolism
While a eating little bit is fine
making them a staple crop
or a predominant part of any diet
has been found to be quite harmful

There is actually a crazy amount of diversity
of these finger grains available in the larger world
but I am not a botanist
and I don't have access
to more than one or two varieties of either
so we'll have to move on

Rice

Rice has its own complex history
and intense genetic diversity
It is the most widely consumed staple food
for over half of the Earth's human population

Rice is an intensely complex subject
diverse in terms of farming practices
and baking qualities
worthy of its own book
that I don't have the time
or authority
to write
but briefly

There are at least forty thousand varieties of rice
but rice is divided into two major races
japonica which is known as short or medium grain rice
and **indica** which is the longer grain varieties
the major difference being starch and protein contents

Brown and white rice are not different grains
The difference between brown and white rice is that
brown rice
or **black rice** or **red rice** for that matter
is whole grain
meaning it still has the bran intact

Rice is not milled in the same way as wheat
The bran is polished off

White rice is the innermost starch
after the bran has been polished off
Haiga rice is where the rice bran is only slightly polished off

Oats

Oats are an ancient grain
also typically in need of de-hulling
They have a wonderfully creamy simple flavor
They are a perfect canvas
and enhance the flavor of any grain
or ingredient they paired with

Oats typically come in three forms
Rolled oats which we typically encounter
in the grocery store as oatmeal
where the grain is smushed to form a flat oval
steel cut oats where the whole grain is cut in half
and **whole groats**
which are the whole oat seed

Barley

Hulled barley is eaten
after removing the inedible outer hull
Once removed
it is called **dehulled barley**
Considered a whole grain
dehulled barley still has its bran and germ

Pearl barley or **pearled barley**
is dehulled barley
which has been steam-processed further to remove the bran
It may be polished
a process known as pearling
Dehulled or pearl barley may be processed into various forms

including flour
and flakes similar to oatmeal

Barley is the cornerstone of beer brewing
specifically malted barley
made from roasted barley to increase its maltose content

Barley flour
malt and syrup are also used in bread making
to increase enzymatic activity

A note on farro and bulgur

Farro is actually an ethnobotanical term
for three species of hulled wheat
typically cooked as whole berries
much like rice

Farro piccolo is typically einkorn
farro medio is typically emmer
and farro grande is typically spelt

Bulgur can be any type of wheat berry
roughly cracked and parboiled
for quicker cooking later

Salt is death and death is a part of life

Salt in bread is not really about flavor
Salt slows the rate of fermentation
by competing with yeast
for water in the dough

Salt is the control
that makes everything possible

Some destruction of the culture is necessary
to make the agents of fermentation stronger

If there were no salt
the yeast would consume the sugars too quickly
and deplete themselves before they could leaven the loaf
leaving a strange texture
and an even stranger taste

The mineral content of certain salts
increases extensibility
so sea salt is ideal
due to its mineral content
Certain sea salts like French gris
or Celtic sea salt
and Trapani sea salt from Sicily
have higher mineral contents
These extra minerals taste salty
which not only helps develop the dough but adds more flavor
when only a minimal amount of salt can be added

Salt reduces oxidization during mixing
helps strengthen dough
and reduces the destruction of carotenoids
that come from mixing
or oxidization
Salt in cooking
can actually increase nutritional content
as well as flavor

Sugar isn't really sugar

Sugar cane is a plant that has tons of nutrients
What we know as sugar is just one part
We separate the white sugar
from the molasses
Much like endosperm and bran
the molasses has all of the nutrients
and the white part
when we consume it
tells our bodies that we're getting those nutrients
Our bodies freak out and want more
but they're empty calories
and as a result
our energy supply is constantly crashing
when we consume these sugars
with white cane sugar and white flour
This is called insulin shock

Sugar isn't one thing
You need
either simple sugars
or complex carbohydrates
to live

White cane sugar
and honey
and fruit
and bread
are all different parts
of the same thing
Some have fructose
Some have dextrose
maltose
sucrose

even lactose is a sugar
and on and on

These sugars
all break down differently
in your body
and have different reactions

Calling white cane sugar
sugar
is reductive and manipulative

In bread making
sugars feed the yeast and bacteria
but this is where it gets funny because
simple sugars
like cane sugar
can actually kill yeast
by fighting with them
for water in the dough
because they're both hydroscopic
just like salt

The sugar that your yeast likes to consume
is the sugar it makes by breaking down starch
This sugar is called maltose

Making a slurry of yeast and water and sugar
or what a lot of bread recipes refer to as
blooming the yeast
is actually killing about half the yeast
which is fine
but you could just use less yeast

I stay away from cane sugar
Slavery is an issue

in the places where cane sugar is harvested
much like chocolate
and sugar is controlled by some of the largest monopolies
in the world

There's always a better alternative

Sorghum is a great substitute for molasses
and there's also maple syrup and maple sugar
and local honey

Raw honey is great for you
because of its antibacterial properties
but it's not so great for sourdough sometimes
because sourdough is benefited greatly by its bacterial content
A little bit will be okay
but it can affect fermentation times
and development

Adding sugars
will increase the hydration of your dough
Sugars act like liquids in dough
They will tenderize or soften the texture of your crumb

Sugars also affect the crust of your bread
The more sugar present in the dough at the time of baking
will make your crust caramelize faster

Fat

In bread making typically
doughs that have fats added
are called **enriched doughs**

Adding fat slows down fermentation
There's less water activity
at different points in your dough
and so everything happens at a reduced rate
but there are ways to make your starter
to get it used to sugar and fat
so that your dough can develop
with more strength
and less sour flavors
despite the longer fermentation time

People make fruit yeasts
often from dried fruit like raisins
to make yeast waters
and feed one-time starters
that are much less acidic
or sour in flavour
and much more suited to enriched breads
than regular sourdough

Similarly
bakers make sweet starters
that are fed with sugars and sometimes fats
and fed in very specific proportions
to work better with enriched sourdough breads
most commonly
for an Italian sourdough sweet bread called pannetone

Fat also leads to tighter crumb structures
The connections in the matrix of the crumb
are slippery from lubrication
and the gaps collapse
This can be adjusted for with more intense mixing techniques
and by using higher protein flours
giving the structure more development early on

And with the addition of sugar
these doughs can get a unique fluffy cloud-like texture
that has a very pleasant mouth feel
like shokupan
and challah

Fat also adds hydration
Butter
olive oil
eggs
all have water content

Fat is really amazing in bread
Eggs and animal fat
or dairy
combined with the nutrients in wheat make a perfect protein
or a complete chain of amino acids

Bread and butter are a perfect protein
and are also
probably for the same reason
delicious

Just remember to source these things directly
from people you trust
There's lots of miserable assholes out there
abusing animals for the sake of their by-products

Adding weird shit

You can put about 30% broken glass in your dough
and it will still rise
But you probably shouldn't do that
Try porridge

What the fuck is **porridge**
It's just like oatmeal
or any cooked cereal mixture
I usually go with a 4:1 water to grain mix
Bring to a simmer
and cook until most of the water seems to be absorbed
and it looks like something you want to eat

Typically
the weight of the porridge
should be 10–30%
in baker's percentages

Cooking the grain ahead of time
and then mixing it into a dough
allows the starches
in the pre-cooked grain
to gelatinize
and hold more water
adding moisture
and structure to the bread
during baking
without making your initial dough
overly hydrated

Cook your favorite cereals in different mixes
with different seasonings and enrichment
Try some shit out

Scalds are the same idea as porridge
a pre-gelatinized starch
but usually not cooked for any period of time

You just pour nearly boiling water
over coarsely ground grains
or even flour
and stir to incorporate

Doing this with flour
creates a supercharged hydration
that will add moisture and flavor to your dough

This could also increase enzymatic activity
Remember
maltose feeds the yeast
Rye is still rye
Einkorn is still einkorn
These things will ferment faster
when added to bread
even as porridge

Alternatively
you can roast theses grains and flours
before scalding them
and making them into porridge

Toasting oats on a baking sheet in the oven until brown
then making oatmeal
adds a rich
crazy flavor
reminiscent of turkey skin

You can also toast and soak seeds
to add to your dough
Ideally things like grains
nuts and seeds
should be soaked
or scalded
about 8 hours before your initial mix
Otherwise they tend to sap moisture from your dough
You can always add more water to the dough in the
beginning
to adjust for this
or if you forgot
or don't want to soak things
but you can only add so much water content to your dough
without changing the structure

Things that are soaking will ferment
which isn't the biggest of deals
especially because you should salt them slightly
to adjust for taste
and that will curb fermentation

Beets and carrots
create incredible unique sweet flavors in bread
Supremely starchy vegetables
like potatoes and squash
make great bread additions
because they act like porridge
infusing extra moisture as the bread develops

Just remember that they all have water content
and will raise the hydration of your dough

I typically roast these vegetables
with oil and salt
then puree them
before adding them into the dough

Dehydrated fruit is preferred for bread making
because of shelf stability
and fructose's effect on dough

The thing about fructose in dough
is that nobody seems to understand
how it works in bread

Fructose is a natural product of fermentation
But adding it to dough can make things tricky

Bananas are an interesting example

Bananas are really interesting in baking
because they act like a 1:1 replacement
for butter
and sugar
and flour
and eggs

One of the first things I learned to bake was cookies
that were just bananas
You just put some chocolate chips and oats in for texture
scoop and bake

So I said to myself
Self
Why can't I make bread the same way
Like banana bread
but like banana bread
that's leavened

So I started experimenting
and what I saw
was that the dough broke down really fast
It wouldn't stay together while fermenting
But just by baking a bit earlier and folding a bit more gently
I got more and more bananas in the recipe
until I was up to 70%

But then I was working with another baker
and he told me
You can't have fresh fruit in a dough
because fructose starts to break down the dough
I told him what I had done and unfortunately
he was so confused
that he just kinda shut down

I think this is an important lesson
The way we perceive things
is fundamentally flawed
We can't always see something as possible
despite the fact
that everything keeps showing us
that as long as we believe
anything is possible
if we can get just out of our own way

When using dehydrated fruit
soaking in water is ideal
You don't need to soak the fruit for very long
although depending on how they're dried
you may want to do it overnight
Personally
I fill up the container my fruit is in with water
and then drain it after about five minutes

I like to season my rehydrated fruit
Seasoning goes a long way
to bring out the best of your fruits' flavor
Just remember certain seasonings
like cinnamon
and ginger
are antibacterial
just like the raw honey
and can affect the fermentation of your dough

Water is just water

(water)

Water is a big ingredient
It will likely be more than half your dough weight
That being said
it's pretty hard to affect
Besides setting the temperature
you can't really do too much to affect its quality
except filter it

Now filtered water is great
Definitely use non-toxic water
But you don't need filtered water
to make bread
Mineral content can actually help
Hard water
or poor quality water is sometimes preferred

(also water)

People say that's the key to bread and bagels
in Philadelphia and New York City
There are tons of other cities that have hard water
and make terrible bagels

There are just as many
if not more
shitty bagels on the East Coast
as there are good ones

Shots fired!

The fluoridation of your water
can affect how your culture develops
because the fermentation process
is heavily reliant upon bacteria
and fluoride kills bacteria
If you notice that tap water isn't cutting it

try boiling it first
or letting it sit out
until the fluoride degases
You'll find this is only an issue
when starting your starter
Once you have a healthy culture
fluoridation shouldn't affect fermentation

Also feel free to use any weird-ass edible liquid
your heart desires
Whey
the leftover liquid that separates from the curds
in acid-set cheeses
has tons of protein and makes great bread

The water from boiling vegetables
has nutrients
that are normally discarded

And who knows
maybe you'll enjoy an orange juice challah one day
I wouldn't
but you're not me

Yeast is hardly an ingredient

It's the presence of god
A great unknowable force
that can hardly be quantified
It is
life itself
Anima
Drive
It's everything that we will never understand
but always feel

To think that we can cultivate it
is to try to control a higher power
Respect is necessary
fear optional

It is everything
but to call it an ingredient
seems wrong
A higher power
a reason to be
seems more appropriate

People always ask me
How can I get a starter
or
I'm looking for a starter
or
I just got a starter from four hundred years ago
And I'm always like

Ok that last part wasn't a question but here we go

Starters
are not a sacred thing
that you get
Yeast
Bacteria
Divine presence
is a gift
that is blessed upon all things

They are present
in and on
almost everything

They will be in the flour
and water
and container
that you use to make a starter
and they will even be on you

Your starter will taste like you
no matter how old it is
or if you got it from someone else
or made it yourself

Assign any romanticism wherever you want
but your starter
is your starter
and also a great unknowable force
whether you like it or not

You cannot make it
You cannot kill it
You cannot be responsible for it
It is greater than your conscious thoughts and desires
It is beyond your guilt and morals

It is something that chooses whether or not to contribute
and above all
It is not something you should worry too much about

Just respect it
and it will respect you

Yeasts are single-celled microorganisms
members of the fungus kingdom
The first yeast originated hundreds of millions of years ago
and 1,500 species
are currently recognized
It's complicated
but

If you wanna get started

You're gonna need a starter

The key here is
just do it

Seriously

Making a starter
is so simple
you'll probably screw it up
because you want it to mean more than it does
just like your first relationship

All you need
is flour
and water
and time
and a container
and time
and patience
and just remember to relax
It's not important what you do

You're a speck in the cosmos
attempting to ferment grain
so you can eat hot bread

It's gonna be fun if you don't overthink it
and it might even be slightly enjoyable
if you do overthink it
if my life is any kind of proof

First
mix flour and water
and that's really it

Seriously
that's all you're gonna do
over
and over again
for the rest of your life

Equal parts flour and water at first
Any kind of flour will do
I prefer whole grain
especially rye

Now the idea behind this
is that whole grain flour
has more nutrients
that the bacteria and yeast
you want to work with like

You're creating a culture
of tens of millions of strains of yeast
and hundreds of thousands of strains of bacteria
that you can work with
to leaven bread

And all you really need to do that
is to mix flour and water
and throw away most of it every 12–24 hours
and feed the remainder of it
more flour and water
every 12–24 hours
and keep doing that
until it's rising and falling consistently
in the same amount of time

Now you'll notice
if you use a translucent container
that from the side
a sort of honeycomb texture
is developing every time you feed it

What's happening is that the bacteria and yeast
are starting to consume the nutrients you feed them
and creating a structure
with the grain
by consuming the sugars in the flour
and producing gas
the same as what's happening when you make bread

What's happening in terms of the consistency
of how your starter
is rising and falling
is that the specific bacteria and yeast
are starting to create an environment
specific to their individual needs

Each time you discard most of the starter
the bacteria and yeast
that survive the great purge
will create an environment
better and better for them
and less habitable
for their nefarious competitors

And the specific microbes
that make shit last
for generations
will create an ideal society
like Atlantis
or the mall

This society will be effective in how it consumes resources
and will keep their culture healthy by creating a unique acidity
that will discourage the growth of harmful bacteria

The age in the rising and falling cycle
or when you use it to leaven bread
because of that acidity
will heavily affect how your bread develops
and tastes

The spectrum of acidity to alkalinity
is called the pH scale
and your dough and starter's pH
is a great metric for how they are doing

Now you could get a pH meter
or you could just assume
that based on how you feed your starter
its pH is roughly where you want it to be

Typically
when a healthy starter is fed
and left at room temperature
it's ready to use in about three hours
but is more ideal for use at about 8–12 hours
when it's hungry again
but still has some moxie left

Just remember
your starter is unique
just like everybody else's

The bacteria and yeast
on your skin
and in your environment
are incredibly unique

and will be different
no matter what you do
so don't get too caught up
trying to create the perfect blend
It's nature
it's a mess
it's already perfect

The more you discard
feed and stir
it's gonna develop
into something beautiful
I promise
okay

Everything is a variable
affecting how the culture
of your starter progresses
The type of flour
The temperature of the water
The temperature of the room
and the temperature of the flour
and on and on and on and on

To maintain consistency
you wanna keep your starter at a consistent temperature
The most common
or simplest to maintain
is room temperature
or 70° Fahrenheit

How you maintain this temperature
changes all the time
because based on your conditions
the room
and the flour

and the water
will all be different temperatures
Just try to use slightly warm water
mix it thoroughly
and keep it covered
in a warm spot

Don't put your starter in anything airtight that can break
The starter will produce gas
and eventually burst the container

It's useful to keep your starter covered
The cover will keep the surface from drying out
and maintain a more even temperature

If you just keep it simple
and see what happens
everything will be fine

If
for some reason it's not working
you can always adjust
the temperature of your room
or the water
or the type of flour

But be patient
it will take time

Just keep feeding it
Try to practice patience

Talk to it
Name it
Take it on a walk

Tell it you love it
but only if you mean it

Please
don't tell anything that you don't love
that you do
and if you do love something
tell it all the time

Hydration is important
A more hydrated starter will ferment faster
and a less hydrated starter
will ferment slower

When you're first making a starter
stick to equal amounts of flour and water
by weight

Once your starter is consistently rising and falling
you can slow down these fermentation periods
by cooling or retarding the starter
typically in the fridge

Cold temperatures slow yeasts' life cycle
Under 45°F they start to fall into dormancy
and after some time
die
but not all of them at once
Again remember
this is a multifaceted thing
It's a whole culture
not one thing
It's a they
not an it

Certain flours like cold temperatures
or do better fermenting in them
Others do not
High percentages of rye
sometimes do ugly things
when left at cold temperatures to ferment
Durum starters do very well being refrigerated
They're great for long periods of time
at cold temperatures
with very low hydration
often referred to as
pasta madre

There's a really interesting low hydration
refrigerated starter technique
called desem
which is the Dutch word for starter
You can read all about this
in The Laurel Kitchen Bread Book
or my personal favorite
The Bread Builders

I can't say this enough
Fuck around and find out
This is one of those rare and great situations
where there are very few negative consequences to your actions

The only scenario
in which your starter may become toxic
is if it develops
bad mold
If your starter ever has white or green mold
you can just discard the moldy part
and feed the not moldy part
If your starter ever turns pink
or bright red

you should throw it out
in its entirety
But don't worry
this mold is very rare

The environment that the lactobacillus are making
is so acidic
that you could take a dump in your starter
and it would be safe to use
within a couple of hours
But for the sake of flavor and texture
I would highly recommend you don't do this

I don't know if you picked this up yet
but I do not think that starters are precious

When someone asks me
where I got my starter
or how old it is
I'm usually not very far from realizing
that I have the sudden urge
to tear my clothes off
and run away screaming
lest I catch their pretension

I think that a starter
that was started one week ago
is just as strong
as one that's four hundred years old

Healthy is as healthy does

Every once in a while
somebody tells me
they killed their starter

This is impossible
Remember
you can't kill it
It's not one thing
it's a whole culture

Some part of a culture
always lives on

Even if you don't feed your starter
for weeks or months
in the fridge
or even at room temperature
all that's happening
is the various bacteria and yeast
are starving
creating a more and more acidic environment
with their decay
But if at any point
you were to discard most of it
and feed what remains
the cycle will start again

The more consistently you feed your starter
in the beginning
the more it won't matter later

You can forget to feed it every once in a while
because you'll have a strong starter
that will rise consistently
and leaven bread consistently

I keep my starter using just rye
equal parts flour and water

When I use wheat
I feed it at about 60–70% hydration

I just scrape out the jar
and whatever sticks to the side
is enough to feed the next generation

There's six million ways to make a starter
You can cultivate very particular concoctions
of yeast and bacteria
but this is the simplest way I know
and in my practice
the most efficient

And if you don't wanna make your own starter
you probably don't wanna make your own bread
cause it's essentially the same process

Discard most of it
and keep feeding what's left

You don't need anything special
just flour
water
and a container

Just keep feeding it
Please
don't give up
The only way you can fail
is to give up

Jim Franks

Mixing doesn't really matter

Or everything matters
but like everything in this process
if you fixate on that
you'll go crazy
and never do anything

Where you put the salt matters
When you add the salt matters
How and when you incorporate the water with the flour
and on and on and on
You have to find the variables you can handle
and focus on affecting those

Try not to change too many things at once
so you can see
what effect each action has on each variable

You don't knead anything

Essentially mixing is oxidization
same as a fire
The more oxygen you introduce
the more combustion takes place
so the more you mix the dough
the more you oxidize the dough
or incorporate air
and while salt mitigates this
when you mix the dough
you're heating up the dough
and reducing flavor

Yeasts grow better
in the presence of oxygen
This means that the more the dough is mixed
the more it will be oxidized
and the more the yeast can grow

You're also affecting the enzymatic activity
by heating up the dough
and supercharging those enzymatic molecules
converting starches into sugar
and cutting up protein chains

Mixing by machine
even a stand mixer
you can really beat up a dough
or over-oxidize it
and negatively affect its development
While you will develop strength
your end result may be overly chewy and stiff
and either too strong
or too weak to continue

You wanna mix your dough enough
that you develop the structure you're looking for
while balancing these other variables
to enable the life force in your dough to thrive

In other words
just enough

Most people will tell you
that gluten needs to be stressed
in order to make great bread
and this is a wonderful theory
but as I said before
gluten is a red herring
and most people
thought that laserdisc was a good idea
so what does that tell you

I like to mix by hand
incorporating the flour and water
and then develop structure
through gentle folding

Let's talk about structure

Everything we've been talking about so far
in terms of structure
is affected by how we handle the dough

The internal structure of bread is called the **crumb**
Open crumb is when there are big holes
Closed crumb is when there are little holes
Irregular structure
is when the holes are different all over

I like to think sideways
Look for the fifth angle

Crumb and crust develop flavor and texture
Mouthfeel is a huge part of eating

Some people like dense stuff
Some people like chewy things
Some like soft open custardy bread
and
everything you do
in terms of development
or touching the dough
is a decision in this direction

Hydration

Hydration is the amount of water
related to the amount of flour

Typically store-bought bread
is hydrated about 10–50%
So it has 10–50% the amount of water
as it does flour
in baker's percentages

Where artisan bread
is somewhere between 60–100%

The hydration affects how the starches will gelatinize
when the bread is baked
hence the glossy custardy crumbs of these breads
versus the dry
sometimes almost uncooked texture
of something like store-bought bread

There's an argument
that hydration at higher percentages
does something for digestibility

My first bread teacher used to say

"You wouldn't cook a cup of rice in half a cup of water
would you?"

I said that to some guy on the train once
and he said

"Isn't that how you make Puerto Rican rice?"

Again
do whatever you want

Enjoy these little bits of freedom
whenever you get the chance

The more hydrated a dough
the more its enzymatic activity increases
so your dough will ferment faster

Different grains will absorb water differently
and even different crops
from season to season
will have different moisture contents
especially if you're working with local grains

Large commodity mills adjust moisture content
and all sorts of grain statistics
like protein
(Jim thinks about gluten as a construct of modern thinking)
*(Jim's eyes roll into the back of his head and get stuck there
for a while)*
by aggregating grains from all over and processing them
to make them hydrate and bake more consistently

Whole grain doughs however
need more water to be softer
and more open
The bran soaks up a lot of water

I hydrate my whole grain doughs between 80–100%
They seem soupy
when they're first mixed
but they develop into something less unruly
as time goes by
like teenagers

When to use autolyse

The autolyse technique
comes from systemic problems in mass production of bread
in France just after World War II
primarily because of the development of mixers
that were more efficient in speed but rougher on the doughs
and the low enzymatic activity of the flour
available in France at the time

Autolyse comes from a time
when French people
were trying to save French bread

French bread sucked
Mostly cause it was too white
but also because of the low enzymatic activity of the flour
and they were fortifying the protein content
with fava bean flour
which was diluting the overall quality of the wheat

The French person
who saved French bread
by inventing the autolyse
was named Raymond Calvel
He wrote a book about it called
The Taste of Bread

Autolyse is just resting the dough during mixing
and not adding the salt and yeast
when you first incorporate the flour and water
Which helped a lot
because it developed enzymatic activity
and allowed the dough to cool down
during the mixing process

But hopefully
if you're reading this book
and believing anything I say
you're using nice grain
from local farms
grain that someone pet a deer near
and if that's the case
you don't have to worry about
fava bean dilution
and reduced enzymatic activity

Freshly milled flour
has incredible enzymatic activity
because it has more of the intact nutrients
necessary for enzymes to develop and thrive
especially if you're talking about whole grain flour
or anything near it
because that shit has crazy microbes to feed enzymes
It's got nutrients that make your culture go crazy
and it will naturally develop
plenty of amylase and protease
the main bread-making enzymes

Adding an autolyse is adding fermentation time
that's unencumbered by salt
or yeast and bacteria
or both

But that's not always beneficial

Withholding the leaven and salt
also develops strength
or dough extensibility
Just by mixing the flour and water
and letting it rest for an hour
you'll notice

the dough becomes very cohesively hydrated
and workable
so it's not useless

I think the reason that most modern bread-making techniques
include autolyse is because they are actually teaching you
how to extensively hydrate very white
or less whole grain doughs

When you mix flour and water the proteins begin to form chains
but this is easier to do at lower hydration
because
the water actually dilutes the protein chain-forming molecules
when hydration is too readily available

When the dough is hydrated at a lower percentage
mixed to incorporation
and then mixed again
with more water
the chains are formed
and then hydrated
rather than being over-diluted the first time
and not being able to find themselves
just like me in my twenties

This is called **bassinage**
which in French means
to bathe the dough

Bassinage is very useful for highly hydrated
less whole grain doughs
because it makes them stronger
and easier to handle

It's also useful when working with coarse flour
that would otherwise resist uniform hydration

Autolyse also shortens mixing times
but if you're not using a mechanical mixer
then well
I think you get it

The thing is
the pause incorporated by the autolyse
is not necessary
or even beneficial in most cases
if you're not trying to boost enzymatic activity

If you're looking to make a more highly hydrated
but malleable dough
you can do the bassinage technique
by mixing your dough completely
and then immediately adding more hydration
and mixing to incorporate again

Another reason
I think that the autolyse
appeals to most bread makers
is because it's more fermentation
and most bakers are under-fermenting
when they're first getting started
but once you learn the signs
and how to push proofing times
autolyse becomes redundant

And this is all part of setting your schedule
Your time is important
If you don't have time to make bread
or don't like how bread takes up your time
you won't keep making bread
So figure out how to set bread making
to your schedule
changing all the variables
to make the stages of active work happen
when you want them to happen
and not the other way around

Wait but how much yeast do I use

If you're using monoculture yeast
Anywhere around 1–5%
should be fine

Just mix it into the flour
or water
at any point in the mix

But you might want to **preferment**
some of the flour in your dough
This is a great way to increase flavor
and the keeping quality of your bread

Often these preferments
are mixed
and then refrigerated overnight
about 8–12 hours before
the bread dough is mixed

When a liquid preferment is made
by mixing flour and water at high hydration
usually around 80–100%
this is called a **poolish**
which is classically used for baguettes

When you mix a stiffer preferment
or one with a lower hydration
usually around 40–60%
it's called a **biga**

Somewhere in between would be **pate fermente**
which would also include salt

I've even seen some bakeries use salt
in their sourdough to reduce the acidity
You can even use an old piece of dough
from any bread dough
as the starter for the next batch
This is shockingly called
the old dough method

With sourdough
typically a starter is used
at around 10–20% of the flour weight
but I've seen people go as low as 5%
and as high as 100%

I use 10% starter for most of my bread

The thing to remember is
that how much starter
or yeast you use
will directly effect fermentation time

It's a major variable
in how you set your schedule
and affects flavor

Using more leavening agent
will speed up your dough's fermentation time

The other factor
is the age of your starter
in its fermentation cycle
and how hydrated it is
Just like with the biga
and poolish
if you use a more liquid starter versus
less hydrated ones
you'll have different flavors

It's all a matter of personal taste
and how you observe your starter
at different stages affects the fermentation
of your dough

With high percentage rye doughs
multistage starters are built over days
often even combined with malt
or scalds
to create perfect conditions
and often the starter is between 40–100%
of the flour weight

When I make 100% rye doughs
I feed my starter
at least 18 hours before I'm gonna use it
and use 20%

There's a lot you can affect here
experiment
and find what works best for you

You just wanna make sure you have enough
when you feed your starter to make bread

For example
when I know I need 200g of starter for the next day
the night before I'll mix

10g old starter
100g flour
110g water
which makes
210g new starter

I like to have a little bit extra
because you never know
and some always sticks to the sides of the container

Temperature

Now the temperature of the water
is the key to setting the temperature of your dough
and the schedule you want for fermentation

You an also
chill your dough
to slow down formation
Most bread makers use the term retard
when referring to refrigerating dough
Retard being French for slow

This is usually done with refrigeration
but you can also move your dough
from place to place in your space
until it ferments at the rate you want it to

You can even leave your dough outside
as long as you keep it covered
to keep out any pesky creatures
that may want a nibble

Your environment is filled with microclimates
and just like with your starter
where your dough is
may affect its fermentation speed
Even where it is in the fridge
may have wildly different temperatures
and differently shaped objects
change temperatures at different rates

Just remember
yeast does not like to be above 110°F
or below 40°F
Under 40°F yeast can hibernate
but it's somewhat unpredictable
and may die off
Above 110°F
it will die off rapidly

I prefer to use my own sense of touch to determine
temperature
but you must keep in mind that I have a very firm grasp
on how my sense of touch is biased

The human body is usually at 98.6°F
Water that feels warm to your skin
is probably close to if not above 100°F

If you want a lesson in this
take the temperature of water until it's at 80°F
You might be amazed at just how cool this feels

For ideal ambient dough temp
I usually aim for an 86°F dough
after mixing
Remember it will cool as it sits out
and is folded and shaped

To figure out how to set your dough temp -
there is a formula
based on the temperature of the space you're in
and the temperature of the flour you're using
in order to find the temperature of the water
However
I cry whenever I see algebra
so I avoid formulas at all costs

Which is kinda odd
cause I usually enjoy a good cry

Bulk Fermentation

Bulk fermentation is the term for the first rise
or initial dough fermentation
before you divide the dough
into the smaller parts
that will become your individual loaves

Folding the dough

When you fold your dough
you're developing structure
in a nice simple way
that allows you to do other things
like check in on fermentation periodically

Seeing how your dough moves and feels
throughout this process
becomes a great metric
for how the dough's strength
and fermentation are progressing

Fold the dough onto itself
by picking it up
stretching it to its maximum extensibility
and sticking it to itself

Try not to bunch the dough up
or pinch it too hard
just pick it up and move it
quickly and confidently

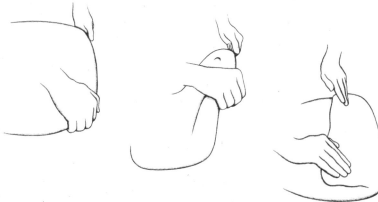

Or pick the dough up
and allow the dough to fall under itself
If you rotate with each fold
this will form a ball

This is called **coil folding**

The idea is that you're stretching the dough
as much as you can
without tearing it
to build strength
so that the dough will have adequate tension
to hold its final shape
and expand upward during baking

This **stretch & fold** technique
is stressing individual protein chains
and then relaxing them
so they can repair themselves
and gain strength each time
just like your muscles
build strength through exercise

Folding is done multiple times
during bulk fermentation
at regular intervals
until the dough has enough strength

How long you wait
in between folding
depends heavily on the type of dough
the temperature
the grain
hydration
development
stage in fermentation
and on and on

I fold at twenty minute intervals
This is typically
the minimum amount of time
you need to wait
between folds
to have the dough relax enough
to be shaped again

With ancient grains
like emmer
einkorn
and spelt
doughs that relax and lose structure quickly

I want to keep them tight
and constantly developing structure
so I try to fold more gently
as many times as possible
while maintaining the twenty minute rests

I fold the way I do
cause I like to
but you
need to develop
your own practice
that fits your dough
and your schedule

You can do this all at once
at the beginning
or in conjunction with folding
by using the slap & fold method
or kneading

Slap & fold is typically done with wetter doughs
that can't be kneaded
or doughs that are heavily enriched
where the fat needs help being incorporated

This is when the dough is thrown against the table
over itself
over and over again

Kneading is when the dough is stretched forward
and pulled back
or simply pushed around the surface it rests on

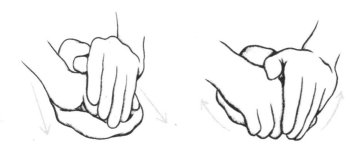

Folding the dough over time
is beneficial
because you are orchestrating
a slow and gentle
calculated death
for a vast society
that is developing within your bread

Every time you touch the dough
you're destroying gas pockets
the yeasts are creating

This culling of gas pockets
and oxidization of yeast
develops fermentation
and diversity of flavors and textures
much in the same way
discarding the majority of your starter
keeps it healthy

It's commonly thought that if you retain
all the air in your dough
your dough will have more flavor
but I find the opposite to be true
The more you allow yeasts and bacteria
to be affected
and to rebuild
the more complex your flavor will be
like pruning a tree to allow for more growth

Setting your schedule

The amount of time that your bulk fermentation takes
is highly variable
mostly based on the temperature of the dough
and the type of grain you're working with

The temperature of your dough is gonna be based on
what temperature it was when you finished mixing
the temperature of the room your dough is in
and the container it's being held in

The shape of the containers
the dough is fermenting in
have different heat dynamics
and different containers have different abilities
to maintain or lose hot or cold energy
based on the materials they're made out of

Metal maintains temperature very well
but typically in extremes
Ceramic loses temperature quickly
Glass and plastic are typically the least reactive

Okay
It's like this
When you wake up in the morning
do you walk around naked
do you put shorts on
or a sweater
I bet it depends on the weather outside
or if you have air conditioning
All these things affect temperature
therefore they're gonna affect your dough

You can
put the dough
at any stage
in a different environment
to slow or speed up the fermentation

You can use refrigeration to slow down fermentation
or retard your dough
The thing about refrigeration
is typically doughs fermented at colder temps
for longer overall fermentation times
are more sour in the way that yogurt is sour
however this acidity is quite pleasant in the right doses
and these doughs have more elasticity
and strength
so people favor them
especially for shaping higher hydration white doughs
that are chronically sticky
while room temperature fermented breads have more
vegetal or vinegar sourness associated with them

With all this in mind
remember the skin of your dough is a factor
You might wanna cover your dough
or oil
or wet it
so that its skin is steeled against
the air in its environment

Also if your dough's skin is too wet
you can use the air to dry it
leaving the dough uncovered
Just remember this will cool it more rapidly as well

When I make bread
my bulk fermentation
at room temperature
takes about four hours
for whole grain wheat and durum
and three hours for whole ancient grains like spelt
emmer
and einkorn

Shaping doesn't really matter

It really doesn't matter
You don't even have to do it
like at all
but it is something we should talk about

We're at that point in your relationship
where it's time to decide
what boundaries are important

I know you're scared
Everything's gonna be fine

We're gonna put the bread in a shape
and hope that it holds that shape
but we have to believe

Okay
stay with me here
This is the fun part for most people

You probably want
to divide the dough
into individual pieces
Shape them once
and let them relax
so you can judge fermentation
and dough strength

Then shape them again
into the shape you want them to be
when they bake

This is where they blossom
from dough into loaves

The thing is
a book is
the worst way to learn this
Shaping is mostly finesse
otherwise known as
ineffable bullshit

I can't teach you this
you need to teach yourself

Shaping isn't based on muscle memory
cause the dough is a little different each time
When you lay the dough down
every time
it will fall differently
When you fold the dough
every time
it will move differently

You have to learn to adjust
and this
in a way
is a gift

You can't do it the same way every time
This is your moment
your practice
your chance to practice patience

Be confident
Think quickly
Accept whatever comes at you
Be your best self
and your worst self
Just be yourself
and stay in yourself
It's gonna be fine
Whatever happens
it's gonna be bread

Don't think about it too much
just try
Do what you can

and don't give up
The only way you can fail is to quit

It can be hard
For me it was hard
For some people it comes very easily
for some people it doesn't
and for most
it takes a lifetime to master

Baking bread in small batches is tough
You have a very limited window to learn to shape
You don't have a hundred loaves to practice on
You might wanna practice on a kitchen towel
or make a dough without yeast
and just practice the movements

Be gentle yet firm
You wanna guide the dough
toward what you want it to do
and not what you don't want it to do
Make little adjustments
and suggest the idea
rather than demand it

Take every action
with just the time
you need

Stay in your body
Take a break from your mind
This is a good time to try acupuncture
or hypnotherapy

Remember that time
is an illusion

and you are and have been everything
so progress is irrelevant
Now try it again

Remember you can do this
You have done it already

Your surface and lube

Traditionally the surface on which bread is shaped and rested
is called a **bench**

Mostly these are made of wood or metal
A lot of people use a cutting board
or just a clean counter

When deciding on a surface
it's important to remember
that your dough is gonna stick to that surface
You want that
to some extent
You need this to shape
You need to lubricate the surface you're shaping on
so that the dough can move
but not so much that it can't catch on the surface
to create tension

I put water on the bench
before dividing and shaping each loaf
and some on my hands
to handle the dough better
if the dough needs it

If you use flour to shape
You're adding flour to your dough
that will not have time to ferment
and when you throw flour around
it affects air quality
just like any particulate

Bakers can suffer from a unique type of asthma
called white lung
that I am personally hoping to avoid
You can alleviate this by wearing a respirator
but I like to just avoid it altogether by using water

Oil also works

You just don't wanna use these three lubricants at the same time
or to switch from one to the other
without cleaning the surface thoroughly
as oil and water naturally separate
and flour and water
or flour and oil will make dough on your surface
and you wanna avoid dough boogers in your bread
whenever possible

To cut and shape your dough
a knife called a **bench knife**
is used

When holding a bench knife
keep it firmly embedded
in the palm of your hand

It's important to remember that this is
an extension of your hand

When I'm teaching people to shape
I encourage them to slam the knife
against the table
to understand
that they need to keep constant pressure
against the bench
or they will leave dough behind

You can also use
a plastic dough scraper
or anything with a firm flat edge
Some people use putty knives
or paint scrapers
which can be found
at almost any hardware store
in various sizes

THWACK!

For my hand and typical loaf size
I like a 6-inch bench knife
with a flat handle

But if the dough is dry enough
you can just use your hands

Size does matter

How you divide your dough matters
How much dough
you put in your pan
or basket
will heavily affect the rise
and shape of your bread

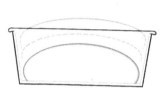

You typically want to fill about 20% of your space
so that the dough can rise to about 75%
and then expand again in the oven

There are all sorts of formulas out there
to establish
how much dough goes in what pan

Some pans come with suggested dough weights
Just keep in mind a white or sifted dough
typically will expand more
and any dough with eggs
will expand much more dramatically
during baking

Typically for a standard 8-by-5-inch loaf pan
I'll divide at 800–900g for a white dough
And about 1000g for a whole grain dough
and about the same
for your average-sized bannetons or basket

Dividing your dough

Lay out your dough
and your scale with
ample space to shape

space to shape

Plunge your knife into the dough
Cut and pull immediately
away from the larger mass of dough

Cut again freeing the piece completely

Place the piece of dough on the scale

Cut additional pieces of dough
as necessary to make weight

Put your dough somewhere
you have room to shape

Push the dough away from you to create tension
and pull it back in a J-shape making small circles

Repeat until the skin is tight
and the dough is a
uniformly round shape

When dividing and shaping
remember
to use simple motions
and always cut completely

Try to handle the dough as little as possible
Try to cut the dough as little as possible
Try to do as little as possible

Take a long deep breath
you're halfway through
It's gonna be bread
It's gonna be okay
and even if it's not okay
that will be okay

You're doing something
One day you will die
Try to enjoy this
It's the fun part

This initial shape is called the **pre-shape**
It's really just another fold
The pieces
are usually placed
in a honeycomb
or grid shape
to rest

Be spatially aware
Think
do I have enough room to move
how is the dough arranged on the table
when it rests and relaxes
will it spill off the table
Bet you didn't think of that did ya

Allow the dough to rest
until it relaxes fully
and is ready to be shaped again

This is called a **bench rest**
For most of my doughs
this is about 20 minutes
but for more slack doughs
or doughs that relax quicker
like rye and spelt
emmer and einkorn
I will pre-shape
and then immediately final shape

This is a great way to see
how the dough is developing
Ideally you see the dough holding its shape
and the pieces
should separate cleanly from one another
as if they were perforated

The way it relaxes
the way it holds its shape
and the way it separates
is a huge marker of fermentation
and dough development

A dough that doesn't separate
is often either over-fermented
or underdeveloped

This is the stuff to pay attention to
How does it feel when you move with it
Is it full of air
is it light or heavy
Is it spreading fast or slow
What do you think all this means
Don't you hate it when people ask questions in a litany

While preshaping can be helpful
and fun
you don't have to do it
It's just a helpful way of organizing

If you think your dough has enough tension
or you just don't like this part
don't do it

You don't have to do
anything
you don't want to

Final shaping

Before you start your final shape
you'll need to set up whatever vessel
you're gonna rest your dough in
for the final fermentation
before baking

I like to roll my dough into a little log
and put it in a pan
but your options here are endless

Often
bread is in a free form
on linen cloth
that is floured and folded
to hold the dough's shape
like with a baguette

Or it's put in a basket
or **banneton**
Bannetons are wicker baskets
sometimes lined with linen
that are usually floured

Most bakers use rice flour
because it has a certain patina

The coarseness of rice flour
resists absorbing moisture
and creates the ideal barrier
between your resting dough
and whatever surface it's supposed to be resisting
but any flour
wheat bran
cornmeal
or semolina
anything with a slightly coarse grind works fine

You can also use any vessel
lined with almost anything
floured or not
as long as the bread can free itself
in the end

You can also roll your bread
in something fun
and visually exciting
like rolled oats
or seeds

This is partially why bread is shaped with flour
as it creates a nonstick quality
for the cloths
or wood
that it will eventually need to be separated from

Traditionally
breads in baskets
are shaped in simple rounds
like the pre-shape
and then placed upside down
or seam-side up
in these baskets
to rise

If you shape bread with water
you will want to flour the surface
or the cloth
as the dough will be wet
and might stick to the basket or cloth

Alternatively
you can place your bread
seam-side down in a oiled pan
to rise

Pans are much more supportive
as the walls
give the dough
a structure to climb

Pans in North America
usually have flared sides
or sides that aren't vertically straight
This sucks for anything
that's not made with high protein flour
that doesn't pull away from the sides
as it bakes

The only reason they're made this way
is that they're easier to machine

While in Europe and Asia
they continued to make pans
the way bakers actually wanted them
in America
the land of fuck the consumer
I'm making money over here
it is nearly unheard of
to manufacture loaf pans with straight sides
If you look around
there's a few bread pans out there with straight-ish sides
and I highly recommend them

Shaping pan loaves

All you're really doing here
is folding in the sides
and rolling up the dough

If you pre-shaped
take the dough and flip it over

It will fall differently every time
you may need to adjust the shape

Stretch out the sides horizontally

Fold the sides in and over each other
so that you form a tapered line vertically
like a collared shirt

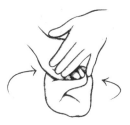

Grab the top of the dough and
stretch and fold it toward yourself

Stick it to itself and push in slightly
creating and tightening your first roll

You want to create a straight line of pressure
with your fingers when you seal each roll

Roll the dough toward yourself
with very slight pressure from the top

Pressing in and down
when you complete each roll

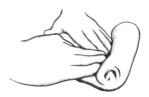

Place your loaf seam-side down
in an oiled pan

The roll will lengthen horizontally each time you roll
so that at the end
the roll will meet the widest part of the taper

Do this until you have a firm roll
that meets the length of the pan

When shaping bread
the goal is to create tension evenly
in as few strokes as possible
but remember
that perfect
is impossible

When you're rolling up your loaf
there's no way you can do exactly the same thing
with each hand at the same time

You'll have to learn to adjust
with each movement
sense
and adapt
to get to even tension
throughout your shape

When I was first learning to make bread
I was an apprentice at a bakery in San Francisco
and I had one day off a week
and I had no friends in the Bay Area
I would go to Golden Gate Park
and rent a row boat on Stow Lake
and take a little picnic
and after that I realised
what a perfect metaphor
rowing was
for shaping bread

If I tried to do the same thing
with both arms consistently
I would just end up going in circles
but if I noticed what my two arms were doing
each stroke
and tried to adjust minutely
to what I had done the stroke before
my brain could turn off and just row

Just row the boat
Don't try to be perfect

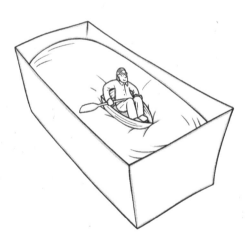

Proofing

Proofing is what bakers call the second fermentation
after the dough has been divided
into individual loaves
and formed into their final shape

Just like with the starter
the bulk ferment
and anything that's fermenting
you can adjust the temperature of the dough
by cooling it in a refrigerator
or heating it up
by placing it in a warm environment

There are proofers
of all shapes and sizes
that regulate temperature
and humidity
to control fermentation
but at home you can just place your bread
in the oven with the light on
or even preheat the oven
to create a slightly warm environment
and if you really wanna get fancy
you can put a pan with some boiling water in there
to raise the humidity

Or if you know a warm spot in the house
where the sun hits at a certain time of day
you can put it there

The air temperature
that maintains ideal dough temperature
is about 70–90°F

If you're making pan loaves
remember
metal retains temperatures very well
It's not really a big deal
if you're proofing at room temperature
but if you put your metal pans in the fridge
they tend to stay cold
even after you take them out
They often need to sit out
to come to room temperature
and allow the fermentation to catch up

It can be beneficial
to let your retarded loaves

adjust to room temperature
before baking

Consider all the ingredients in the dough
If your dough is full of fat
any fat that turns to a liquid
above a certain temperature
could melt
and the dough could fall apart
at high temperature proofing

How to tell when your bread is ready to bake

Essentially
you want your loaf to double in size
That's basically it
but beyond that
there's a whole host of crazy metrics
about
how it should jiggle
what the skin should look like
and if you poke it
how it should react
but
how would you like it
if someone poked you
just to see how you react

When I make bread
I wanna see that the dough
has risen significantly
has a very jiggly jiggle
and doesn't have any big bubbles on the surface

I don't like the poke test very much
for what I feel are obvious reasons
but what you're looking for
when you poke dough
sigh
is that the dough doesn't spring back
and fill in the indentation
too quickly

What's too quickly
I've never been able to get a good answer
but I think
that bread is ready to be baked
when it doesn't spring back at all
However this could also mean
that your yeast and bacteria
are completely exhausted
and it's too late

Once you know how much dough goes into your pan
or basket
you'll have a pretty good idea
how much you wanna see it fill up
said pan or basket
before it's ready to bake

Sometimes large bubbles will appear
on the top of your loaf
This is fine
It might mean your dough needs more time

You can pop them
but ideally
these will dissipate as the loaf proofs

If they don't
you might need to shape with a bit more tension
next time

Scoring

When your bread is ready to bake
you want to cut the surface
following the the strongest point of tension

This is called scoring
You can use any kind of sharp edge
but typically this is done with a **lame**
pronounced with a long a
like in the word llama
A lame is a double-sided razor blade
mounted on a thin flat piece of metal
so that the blade is curved

With a round
or a loaf in a pan
I cut a slightly rounded line
like a smile
because the shape of your loaf
is slightly curved

What you're doing here
is releasing tension
that you created
based on
how the bread is going to expand
during baking
so that the bread can expand
in the way you want it to

Think about where the tension is
in your shape
and where do you want it to go
as it expands

You're looking for the ridge
where the tension is at its apex
on your loaf

Once you get a hang of how the dough expands
you can shape and cut the dough
in different ways to get it to be whatever shape you like
after its oven spring

It's very important
to score quickly
especially when cutting wet dough
If you hesitate
at all
the blade will drag the dough with it
and cease to cut further

You wanna avoid cutting down
into the bread
deflating the loaf
so cut at a 45° angle
to the plane of your surface

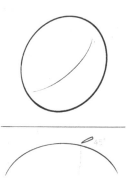

If you're having trouble
try drawing your bread shape
from an aerial view
and then draw the lines
as you want them to look on your loaves

Draw it first and then
immediately walk over to your loaf
and cut that sucker
Bet you'll be surprised

Don't hesitate
If you're stuck
or you're getting frustrated
in any of this stuff
just stop

Turn around
take a deep breath
then
turn around
and do it immediately
without thinking

If you notice yourself thinking
remember
that's stupid
Thinkin never got nobody nowhere

Turn around and try it again
It works

Sometimes
I score the dough
with scissors
when the dough is too wet
or covered in something
that will hinder the lame

Jim Franks

Baking

Time

Typically bread is baked between 350° and 1000° Fahrenheit
for anywhere between 10 minutes and 24 hours
I can't just tell you
how long to do it

Are you exhausted yet
Imagine how the bread feels

You're gonna have to try some shit out
Look at your bread while it's baking
Play with time and temperature
Figure out what works for you
and the bread

You can buy a thermometer
and stick it in your loaf
checking for the desired temp
I think this is weird but if you want to
it's gonna be around 200°F internally
when fully cooked

I like to feel the heft of the loaf
feel how much weight the dough lost
during baking
and I give it a good thump on the bottom
and listen to how it sounds

A well-baked loaf will feel light
and sound hollow

Also
how does the crust look
Is it dark enough for you

If not
put it back in for minute or two

The thing about ovens

They don't really work

Different ovens have different heating elements
in different places

Home ovens most commonly heat from the bottom
but sometimes the heating element is at the top
You can do some research
to find out what models do what
Some even have top and bottom heating elements
that heat up at the same time
This is preferable
if you can find them
cause
you want the most even heat possible

The thing is
nobody builds ovens
to work well
No oven big or small
keeps perfectly consistent heat
throughout the space
partially cause it's too difficult to engineer
and partially cause big appliance conglomerates
don't think you're smart
and don't care about your time
or well-being

It's ideal to rotate your loaves
part way through baking

Sometimes ovens are built with a convection setting
Convection means that a fan
blows the air around
and keeps heat evenly distributed
during baking
This isn't ideal for bread
The air dries out the crust
inhibiting expansion

Very few home ovens go above 550°F
Most don't go above 500°F
and the heating elements in ovens
are usually the first thing to break
It's helpful to get a sense of where your oven is performing
You can buy an oven thermometer
or try things out and adjust
and like all things
it will change

Change is the only constant in the universe

Bread likes it steamy

To avoid caramelizing the crust
too early in baking
so the loaf can expand
it's helpful to add steam to the oven
when the bread goes in

What's happening when we bake bread
is the starches are gelatinizing
The yeast and bacteria
are going crazy
doing what they've been doing
the whole fermentation
but in one last final
glorious push
called the **oven spring**

Steam is hard to maintain in home ovens
The way they heat up
dries out their environment
and vents moisture

Bread ovens can inject steam
and have special valves to release air
when you want to vent the humidity

But you can produce steam
in a variety of ways

You could
make a dome with tin foil
over your loaf pan

Remember that your loaf is gonna expand
and you don't want it to stick to the foil

You can also bake your bread in a dutch oven with the lid on
Or putting anything oven-safe
over your bread
while it's baking

bread goes here

To vent the steam
take off whatever cover you have created
halfway through the baking time
to allow the crust to set

Temperature

If you bake something at lower temps
like 350°F
it's usually gonna have a softer crust
with lighter color
and a softer crumb
when it's finished baking

Lower temps aren't ideal for higher hydration bread
Even though the crust would be caramelized
the inside wouldn't be cooked

Lower temps are great for enriched loaves
where otherwise the crust would burn
because of the sugars present

Using a lower temp
like 350°F
these enriched doughs often need to bake
for around 30–40 minutes
depending on size
and atmospheric conditions

When you're making higher hydration breads
and want a soft but fully set inside
and a hard crispy crust outside
beautifully colored like every shade of the dawn
you wanna bake at a higher temperature

If you have an oven
that goes to 1000°F
do it

If you're baking in a conventional oven
you wanna preheat the oven
as hot as it goes
and drop the temperature slightly
when you put the bread in
like 500°F
to 450°F

Another thing to remember
is that when you open an oven that is preheated
you lose heat through that opening very quickly
so be aware and work quickly
when you need to check on your bread
to vent steam
or rotate it

Large industrial ovens
or wood-fire ovens typically have stone hearths
These maintain temperature very well during baking
radiating consistent heat into the bread
This is often simulated at home with baking stones
or loading ovens with bricks
or baking in preheated cast iron
like a Dutch oven

When I bake bread at home
I preheat the oven to 500°F
and cover the loaf pans in tin foil
When I load the bread in the oven
I turn it down to 450°F
I take the tin foil off after 23 minutes
then I bake it for another 15 minutes
rotate the bread
and bake it for 7 to 8 more minutes

The bread might be out of the oven but it's still cooking

When you first take your bread out of the oven
the crumb hasn't set yet
especially with high percentage rye breads
Often rye breads will take 12–24 hours to set

I have seen people who cut rye right away
and it was fine
I've seen others do it
and it was all gummy
Life's a mystery

There's a lot of steam
still being produced inside your loaf

If you cut your bread right away
and put the crumb
cut side down
you will probably see a puddle form

The bread is seeping moisture
If you let it cool
for 1–24 hours
the crust will season the crumb
and the crumb will set

But
if you have enough people
to eat the whole loaf while it's hot
bread that fresh is incredible

It's important to cool your bread
with air circulating underneath
A simple wire rack will do
or you can prop your loaf
up against something

Keeping it fresh

After baking
keep your bread
cut side down on a clean surface
or in a paper bag

The bag will get greasy
even without oil in the bread
because it's staling
expelling moisture

Your bread is breathing
It's alive

Keeping bread in a sealed plastic bag
will retain this moisture
leading to a softer crust
but also
sometimes
leading bread to mold quickly

Ambient humidity will soften crust as well
When I bake in my apartment
in the summer in Chicago
I have to keep my windows closed
to keep my loaves' crusts crispy
and when I used to live in St. Louis
and put my bread in plastic bags
the bread would mold almost immediately

To create different textures of crust
bakers use various glazing techniques
brushing their freshly baked loaves crust
with everything
from boiling water to butter

You can freeze it
but I don't recommend refrigeration

Bread keeps from molding in the fridge
but it changes texture completely
because it's actually staling much quicker

You can thaw a whole loaf
at room temp
or in the oven

I slice bread before I freeze it
then I can just toast slices
whenever I want bread

What fresh means

The first bakery I ever worked at
took all the bread
out of the oven and just cooled
and froze it

The next morning
they would load frozen bread in the oven
inject tons of steam
and heat it till it was defrosted
Then they would sell it as fresh
and while I think this was extremely dishonest
people loved that shit

They did that cause nobody goes to a bakery
at five in the evening expecting fresh bread
but if you wanna have fresh bread
in the morning

you need to work at night
and working at night sucks

Now the really funny thing is
ha ha
high hydration sourdough bread
made with fatty
local flour
is moist and flavorful
for at least a week
and most people are toasting slices

Why the hell is everyone so intent on getting the freshest bread

Stale bread is ideal
for so many different recipes
Wanna make bruschetta
You're gonna bake that shit in oil
You don't need bread fresh out of the oven

Wanna make french toast
or bread pudding
Stale bread is gonna absorb that liquid
much better

Making a grilled cheese slathered in mayo and butter
well you get the picture

There's a million things to do with stale bread
but bread
especially artisan sourdough
lasts and is fresh
so much longer
than most people are used to
and some breads get even better after a couple of days

People even rehydrate bread
brushing slices of it
with water or egg whites
before toasting
or rinsing a whole loaf of bread
and baking it again
to reverse the staling process

The next time you're thinking of asking a baker
if their bread is fresh
or if you can get a discount for day-olds
remember that most people who make food for a living
from the farmers to the cooks
don't get paid enough money to live
and that we as a global society
throw away at least 40% of what we produce

The food system we live in is broken
and the only way we can fix it
is to adjust our expectations
and
you know
get rid of money

You made it

Now let me tell you a little secret

You don't have to do any of this
to make bread

You can find a new way
or follow anyone else
and it will still be great

And I can't say this enough
Nothing really means anything
That is to say that
nothing is black and white

Well this book is
but you know what I mean

Everyone will try to tell you
that this is for this
and that won't work for that
Try to be skeptical
Keep an open mind

Recently
I found a new source of einkorn
from a very small mill

The flour was this beautiful texture
so silky
full of fat and moisture

When I made a fist with the flour in my hand
it formed a solid clump
that held until I poked it apart
with my finger

Just beautiful
The holy grain
And when I made bread with it
everything about the process
was different
I couldn't fold it
without tearing
It seemed over-fermented
from the beginning
It was a disaster

Even though
the dough never came together
I scooped the slop into a pan
and baked it just to see what happened
It was over-proofed but
only a bit too dense for me

So I tried hydrating it less
and less
every time
until I could shape it

But the dough never held together
I got to about 50% hydration
and still
it wasn't the texture I wanted

I wanted to be able to shape it
cause it's my favorite part of the process
but when I gave up on shaping the bread
and I paid less attention to the hydration
and instead paid attention to fermentation
the bread rose better

The less time I gave it in bulk
and the hotter I fermented it
the better texture I got

Treating the einkorn like rye
no shaping
quick fermentation
in the end
I got a beautiful texture
and a flavorful crumb

This einkorn and me
we wanted two different things

I needed to let it grow
the way it wanted to grow
It wanted to make the bread
it wanted to make
and in the end
I realised
I needed to learn how to listen to it

And to me
relationships are the same
There is no perfect partner
There is no perfect bread
You just need to figure out what
you're willing to do
to make it work

Cause the thing is
making bread is not hard
Making perfect bread is hard
It's impossible

But making great bread is possible
It takes time
It takes respect
It takes love
It's not something
that's ever really done
but anyone can do it

The reason that
I make bread
that people love
is that I truly love
making bread

The good days and bad
I wanna be with it
I wanna do the work
I wanna stay with bread forever

And if you can figure out
how to love making bread
how to give yourself to it
and be yourself with it
you'll make
some of the greatest bread
the world has ever tasted

Just remember
fucking up is normal
The trick is learning how to fix things

Thanks youse

I would never have written this book
without
Shaina Hoffman
who still introduces me as writer
to anyone who will listen

Ryan Davis
who gave me the first
best job I ever had

Bill MacKay and Cheryl Bittner
who always see the most in me

Patchwork Farms
who gave me a place to be

Matt Kedzie
who never thought twice
about treating me nice

Hazim Tugun
who always answered my questions
even though I kept saying his name wrong

Douglas (Doug) Ryan
who showed me how he made bread
& told me I had to make my own starter

And Anna Nance
who told me writing this book was my destiny

About the author

Jim Franks lives
In Chicago Illinois
where he is trying to save the world
one loaf at a time